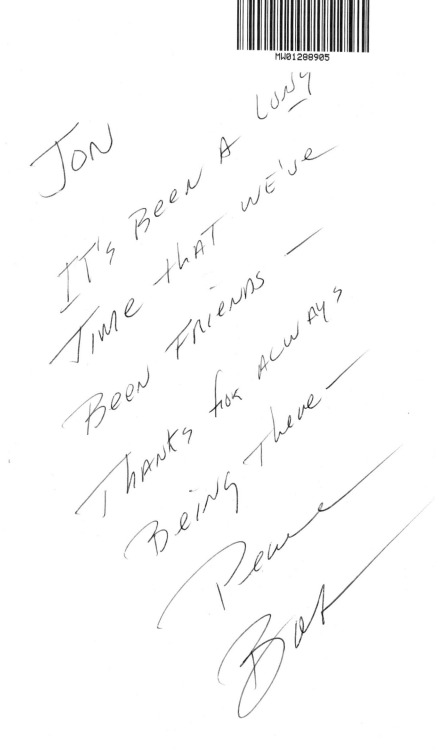

JON

IT's BEEN A LONG
TIME THAT WE'VE
BEEN FRIENDS —
THANKS FOR ALWAYS
BEING THERE —

Peace

Bret

Beating The Time Bandits

BEATING THE TIME BANDITS

How to Transform
Time into
Success, Wealth & Happiness

By

Robert R. Hartung

Published by:
Performance GAINS, Inc.
Hoffman Estates, IL 60169
847.490.8402
www.performancegains.com

To order additional copies contact us at
books@performancegains.com

**Beating the Time Bandits
How to Transform Time into
Success, Wealth & Happiness**

Cover: Design and illustration by Dennis M. Francis

First Printing: October 2006

ISBN- 978-1-4303-0942-0

Printed in the United States of America

Dedication

This book is dedicated to Judi, my wife of 25 years. You are my soulmate and a source of constant encouragement. Thank you for letting me steal so much of your time to complete this project. Also, my three sons, Kyle, Geoff and James; I thank God every day for our time together.

A portion of the proceeds from the sale of this book will go to fight Autism.

Beating The Time Bandits

Contents

Beating The Time Bandits

Introduction

There have been numerous books written about how to achieve personal and career success. If you are like millions of other "success junkies," names like Brian Tracy, Anthony Robbins, Earl Nightingale, Napoleon Hill, Jim Rohn, and Deepak Chopra are probably household names to you. As a matter of fact, there have even been movies made on the subject. I dare say, there have been even more books written about how to succeed in life. Books on goal setting, personal growth, personal achievement, personal development, etc. abound. An entire industry sprang up that now includes the sale and distribution of audiotapes, CDs, videotapes, seminars, workshops, etc. This industry generates billions of dollars every year all for the benefit of people just like you and me; people that have a desire to become better than they are; people that know there is more to life and want to figure out the "secret" to getting it.

As a professional trainer, facilitator and coach for many years, this book is my attempt to help you find your "pot of gold" at the end of the rainbow. It is my interpretation of what I have learned throughout my career and I hope you will find it helpful. Before I begin, let me first provide you with some background.

Beating The Time Bandits

For most of my working adult life I have been in some form of management or leadership position. I was always charged with getting results for my employers and, since starting my own "Resulting" practice 10 years ago, my clients. I have been blessed with working with some very successful, knowledgeable, and motivated individuals. It has been my privilege to work with some of the best mentors a person could hope for.

The first third of my career began in the retail business. I worked for Sears when there was still Roebuck, the customer was always right, and "Satisfaction was always guaranteed."

Following this 13 year, 3 month, 3 weeks, and 4 days experience, I made a career change to the highly competitive, "the customer is *never* satisfied" transportation industry. This was an exciting, fast paced industry and I learned volumes about training, motivating people, managing multiple priorities, problem solving, and much more. The work was somewhat gratifying but more often just plain frustrating. I never truly felt in control, someone else always seemed to be in charge. I realized that I was hampered by the demand to follow someone else's agenda. I also recognized that my greatest pleasure came when I was able to help my employees grow and achieve personal success. It was this realization that led me to start my own business in 1996.

My company is Performance *GAINS*, Inc. and I specialize in helping individuals and companies "*Transform Their Personal & Business Dreams into Reality*." I have never been happier. I wake up every day knowing that my work will benefit others in a positive way. I am in the business of truly making a difference in the world, one person at a time.

Along the way I have had many successes and triumphs. I have also suffered my share of failures and this is the good news. You see, it is from these adversities and setbacks that I learned my most valuable lessons.

This book is in a large part the direct result of what I've learned throughout my career. I learned what works in business and, more importantly, what works to ensure personal success in whatever you desire from life.

I discovered that to be successful in anything: sports, relationships, career, financial independence, health, business, etc. you need to do four things and do them consistently and do them well.

Beating The Time Bandits

You need to:

- Create a *PLAN*
- *IMPLEMENT* your plan
- *MEASURE* your progress & results
- *ADJUST* your activities to stay true to the plan and reach your goals

It really is that simple. Four simple steps: Plan, Implement, Measure and Adjust. Yet, as simple as this sounds, I am constantly amazed at how people overcomplicate the entire process.

I have learned that most problems are solved and great achievements are possible with a simple approach. And frequently the simple solution is the best solution. Let me offer an example.

During the early days of the Space Race, NASA spent millions of dollars to have a pen designed that would perform flawlessly in the weightless conditions of outer space.

The Fisher Pen Company eventually solved the problem by designing a pressurized ballpoint pen. Russia, our competitors and at the time leaders in the race for space dominance, had a *simpler* solution - they used a pencil!

Introduction

Simple, effective, and at a cost (I assume) much less than the millions of dollars we spent.

Beating The Time Bandits

It is my intention with this book to help open your eyes and teach you how simple yet powerful these concepts are. When applied, I am confident they will lead you to greater success, happiness and wealth. It is my intention to help you discover a *simple* solution to what seems to be an insurmountable problem - squeezing more time from every day.

To accomplish this I will:

1. Explain how defining your personal Values and Vision will change the way you look at life and how you spend your time.

2. Show you how setting realistic goals will help you create meaningful time strategies.

3. Help you create real balance in your life that will increase your effectiveness and ensure that when you reach your goals you will be happy and fulfilled.

4. Show you how to identify and arrest your most common "Time Bandits," those daily time wasters that keep you from feeling satisfied and in control.

So, what are we waiting for? Let's get started. Times a wasting!

Time, Your Most Valuable Asset

Just why is Time so valuable? Before we get started, it is important that you understand several simple concepts about time.

First, it is *inelastic*. It can't be stretched, rewound, slowed down or sped up. As a friend of mine frequently says, "…it is what it is." Every day comes packaged with 24 hours or 1440 minutes or 86,400 seconds. No more, no less. We all have the same amount of time to work with. Therefore, we must be very careful how we use this precious commodity or it will simply slip away, vanish, and be gone forever.

Second, Time is *irreplaceable*. Once you use it, you lose it. We can't go to the copying machine and make extra copies to use over and over again. As you read this sentence, the seconds are ticking away, tick tock, tick tock, tick tock See how I just wasted your time?

Annoying isn't it? On a daily basis this occurs over and over again; people wasting our time. Sadly, if you are like most people, you do little if anything to stop it. By the time you finish this book you will have the resources necessary to regain control of your time. It will be up to you to take action.

Finally, Time is *unstoppable*. There is no hold or pause button on your daily time clock.

15

Beating The Time Bandits

Time is very much like the Duracell bunny in those cute TV commercials; it just keeps on going and going and going. Ticking away, tick tock, tick tock, tick tock.

When taken in totality, it is obvious why Time is truly our most valuable asset. Let's examine this a little more closely.

Time Management Portfolio

Imagine that every second of every day has a dollar value attached to it, say $1.00. Every day, at the stroke of midnight $86,400.00 is deposited into your personal Time Management Portfolio (TMP). This is your daily operating fund. You can spend or invest this "money" anyway you choose. It is entirely up to you; however, this "bank" has some interesting rules.

1. You are not allowed to rollover any unused balances to the next day.
2. Every day the account is emptied of whatever unused balance remains.
3. The only way to grow your assets is to invest in activities that move you closer to your Long Term Goals.

Think of your TMP as an offshore account in the Cayman Islands. By properly investing your time allocations these "investments" grow and reap huge benefits. The rewards are the results of your lifelong accomplishments. In business,

Return on Investment (ROI) is one way to measure the success or failure of a company. ROI is a calculation of how much profit you make based on your financial investment.

According to Brian Tracy, in your personal life a comparable measurement of success is your Return on Energy or Effort (ROE). In other words, the more wisely you invest your time or "sweat equity" towards the accomplishment of your goals, the more your TMP will grow. It is within this portfolio that your real personal wealth will accumulate.

Everyone has a TMP. How is yours performing? If you have never reviewed your Time Management Portfolio, let me walk you through the process.

Let's begin by reviewing the three key components of your profile. These areas are your personal and professional: *Values, Vision and Goals.*

Your Core Values

The first thing you need to do is define your personal Value system. You see, your Values or beliefs define how you see things in your daily life, how you make your choices. Your Values determine the importance you place on your relationships, activities, possessions, and yes, your time. Your Values act much like a pair of prescription glasses. Depending on your prescription you "see" the world in a unique and distinct way. When viewing the world while wearing your glasses you see things clearly; everything is in focus. If you don't wear your glasses or if you were to use someone else's, things would appear distorted, fuzzy or out of focus.

Apply this concept to politicians. It might be said that Liberals and Conservatives have different prescription lenses; therefore they "see" things very differently. When people disagree or express dissimilar opinions you get to see a reflection of what they believe; a glimpse of their Values. This doesn't mean that one is right and the other is wrong; it simply means that their "point of view" is different. This frequently can result in conflict. In the simplest terms, there's no right or wrong, only different Values.

Beating The Time Bandits

This is an important concept because people often look at the world wearing glasses with the wrong prescription. People frequently see things as others want them to see it not as they themselves need to see it. Just as no two people are exactly alike, no two people have exactly the same Value system. By understanding your Value system and recognizing that we are all different, it becomes easier to understand how these "lenses" can affect our choices.

Here are some common Values:

Integrity	Family
Honesty	Loyalty
Religion	Happiness
Financial Security	Love
Generosity	Perseverance

Take out a sheet of paper (Appendix II) and make a list of the people and things you value most. Think of the role models in your life. Think of the people you most admire, trust, and go to for advice. This list might include people from your past or present. You may not know them personally but you do know of their accomplishments.

Understanding Your Core Values

This list will provide you with clues about what you hold most sacred; your Core Values. Review this list carefully and begin to identify the traits that represent your personal belief system. Identify and rank your top five Values. This is important when it comes to setting goals relative to your long term TMP. If your goals create internal conflict with your Values it is unlikely you will ever achieve them and, if you do, rest assured it will be a hollow victory.

Examine your list. Ask yourself if you live by these Values every day. If you do, great, however, if you don't, immediately create a plan to improve. This is important so that you become the person you are meant to be. Keep in mind that your Values are not what you *say* they are. Your true Values are defined by your actions. Ask yourself if others see you the way you want to be seen.

> *"What you do speaks so loudly I can't hear a word you say"*
> **Ralph Waldo Emerson**

Your Core Values act as powerful lenses; they help you stay focused on the clear Vision of your future and enable you to see what is most important to you. Don't allow yourself to become distracted or convinced to act in any way that conflicts with your conscience. Commit today to only do the things that are in your best interest as seen through your lenses. Please do not misinterpret this to mean you should become selfish, uncaring or uncooperative. Your actions should, as much as possible, be a true reflection of your inner self and keeping you on the path to happiness.

Getting people to see things in new ways is a common practice used to market new ideas. It is how advertisers get us to buy products or services. A good marketing campaign can create the *perception* of a need that may not be real. Let me offer an example.

Years ago I worked in the transportation industry. At the time, Federal Express was handling thousands of packages for overnight delivery. You may remember their ads: *"When it absolutely, positively must be delivered overnight by 10:30AM..."* They did an outstanding job of getting shippers to "see" a need that was not nearly as big as it was. Perception became reality. Of the millions of packages they delivered each year, how many of them *really, really,* needed to be delivered *"...by 10:30 AM the next morning...?"* To tell the truth I don't have the answer. What I do know is that if I had a dime for every package I saw sitting *unopened* days or weeks after FedEx delivered them I would have a substantial surplus in my *cash bank account.*

You see, FedEx convinced much of the business world to look at how packages were shipped through a different set of lenses. They persuaded them to wear their prescription glasses. They convinced companies that faster was better; even if it cost 150-200% more than standard 1-3 day delivery which worked just fine in many cases. It was brilliant and it forever changed how companies viewed transportation. They made millions of dollars because they convinced the business word that no one could do it better. Perception became reality.

To maximize your TMP, learn to filter out anything that will cause you to waste your daily allotment of $86,400. This includes people with different Values, and people that want to change your Values.

"Until you value yourself, you won't value your time. Until you value your time, you will not do anything with it."
M. Scott Peck

Your Vision, Your Future

Your Vision

Now let's take a look at the future and begin to create your Vision. This is where you start to see your world more clearly by looking through your personal lenses. Things will begin to come into sharper focus.

Consider your Vision to be a panoramic picture of the future. It will cover a lot of territory and it needs to be a broad snapshot of what you wish to accomplish with your Time, the investment that makes up your TMP.

To assist you in creating this image, visualize yourself standing on a mountaintop and all around you see your future as a vivid, 3D picture. This image should include your personal, business and financial hopes and dreams. It should represent how you *want* the future to look, not what you *think* it will look like. For this exercise, don't worry about whether or not you have the resources or capabilities to attain it. Take as much time as necessary to get this image perfectly clear in your mind.

Once you have this image in your mind, describe the scene as clearly as possible on a piece of paper. Capture in your own words what you see in this depiction of your perfect future. Take as much time as necessary.

(Appendix III)

When you are finished, you should have a better understanding of your true Vision for your life. One of the primary reasons for defining this Vision is that you will be more willing and likely to invest your Time in the activities that will generate the greatest returns into your TMP.

Your Vision will serve two other purposes. First, you will have a powerful tool to keep you focused and headed in the right direction. Much like the needle on a compass, you will always know where you are headed and it will be easy to get back on course if you become lost. All you need to do is look at your compass - your Vision. Trust in yourself and have confidence that you know better than anyone else where you are headed and your Vision will guide you safely home.

Second, your Vision will define where you are going to spend your time. In a sense it defines your "sandbox."

Let me explain what I mean by your sandbox. Since it's founding in 1927, the Gerber Company has had a clear Vision of the company direction. Their Vision is reflected in the company slogan: *"Babies are Our Only Business."* Every product and service they sell have one thing in common - babies. They know what "sandbox" they are playing in and they do it extremely well. Put simply, a clear Vision will prevent you from going where you don't belong.

Your Vision, Your Future

Once you have this picture of what *your* future will look like, you can proceed to the next step, defining how you will focus on the key issues that are most important to reach it. By doing this, you will be able to maximize your TMP and ultimately, your future success and happiness.

Beating The Time Bandits

SMART Goal Setting

Consider your Vision to be your lifelong ambition, the grand daddy of all goals. It will become a strong foundation upon which you will build a series of smaller, Long Term Goals which are more manageable. If you have the ability to see 3, 5, 10 or more years into the future, by all means do so. I suggest creating specific plans or goals for the next 18-24 months and constantly review and update them as you achieve them. Of greater importance is to understand that you need to know where you want to end up tomorrow so you can plot your course today!

Think of this step as looking at your panoramic picture and "zooming" in on several key features. Examine it carefully. Take your time. What do you see? Ask yourself thought provoking questions such as:

Is this really what I want?

How important is it that I achieve this?

How do I feel when I think about it?

Am I 100% committed to getting it?

What am I willing to sacrifice to reach this goal?

How much of my $86,400 daily allowance will I invest to obtain it?

By answering these and other questions you will begin to invest every cent of your daily allowance toward the successful accomplishment of your Long Term Goals and ultimately your Vision.

"All that we are is the result of what we have thought. The mind is everything. What we think we become."
Buddha Quote

SMART Goal Setting

Goal Setting and Goal Achievement

In order for you to set up the best defense against failure, you need to make certain that your goals are clearly stated using the SMART goal setting process. SMART goals take the ambiguity out of what is to be accomplished. What are SMART Goals[1]? They are:

1. Specific
2. Meaningful
3. Achievable
4. Resource committed
5. Time Definite

Here are instructions for setting SMART Goals. (See Appendix IV)

Goals need to be *Specific*. To have the greatest impact goals must be stated in very specific terms. Part of this specificity includes some form of measurement. Stating your goals using measurable terms will help you track your progress, good or bad, and will keep you headed in the right direction. Avoid vague and ambiguous words like "better" or "improve." Instead state what "better" is e.g. "increase my income $5000 more than last year" or "maintain a 50%

---

[1] There are several variations and definitions of SMART Goals. The version here is one I have created and find very helpful.

improvement over the last quarter." Research shows that when activities are measured, results dramatically increase.

Goals need to be *Meaningful.* If you are going to achieve your goal and become successful, you must work hard and make sacrifices. Therefore, there must be something in it for you! What will be your reward for accomplishing your goal? How will you be changed? What are the ramifications of *not* completing this goal?

You need to fully understand and desire the benefits of achieving your goal. Take time to answer these questions and, on a daily basis, refer to these expectations to keep yourself motivated.

Goals need to be *Achievable.* Meaningful goals require sacrifice; they require you to go outside of your comfort zone and cause you to "stretch." If you will achieve something by just "showing up" it is not really a goal. However, avoid the tendency to reach too high or expect things to happen too fast thereby creating failure and disappointment. This will be de-motivating and, constant failure will cause you to lose your desire to win and less inclined to set future goals.

Take time to consider possible obstacles and develop alternative solutions. On your journey of goal achievement, you will surely encounter problems; however, this exercise will help you maintain focus and be prepared with viable alternatives. Considering these potential obstacles, describe why you will still work to reach your goal. State as many reasons as possible.

You need to commit all your available *Resources* to achieve your goals. What knowledge and skills will you need to acquire and what people can you engage in order to help you achieve your goal? What financial commitments and personal sacrifices must you make to successfully complete your goal? How much time will be needed to reach your goal?

Take time to think this through and create a plan to use everything and everyone at your disposal. If appropriate, create two realistic budgets. One based upon the total amount of time that will be required to reach your goal. Will it take hours, days, or weeks? Plan accordingly. Second, create a financial budget based on monetary commitments that may be necessary.

Goals need to be *Time Definite.* Goals have a beginning and an end; they are action orientated. List every step needed from now until completion. Include dates, times, places, deadlines, specific tasks, etc, for each item and then prioritize this list.

Keep in mind that the resources allocated to achieve a goal can significantly impact your time lines. Once completed, this becomes your Action Plan. Be prepared to follow it until the completion of your goal.

This process for setting and achieving goals is a proven method and should not be taken for granted. The most successful people have written goals and a plan for success, happiness and wealth that reflects these principles. Never forget that if you can't see where you are going it is only a matter of time until you become disoriented and lose your way. Fortunately, clear, written goals can serve as your "investment guide"; enabling you to invest your time wisely.

As you begin to focus on the issues that are most significant to you and the attainment of your Long Term Goals, something amazing will happen. You will start, slowly at first, to gain control of your TMP. You will discover that you really do accomplish more every day. This occurs, not because you really *have* more time (after all, that's impossible), but because you are centered on the activities that are most important to you; the things in your life that have real meaning and purpose; the things that you visualized in your panoramic view of the future. Your time investment will start to pay dividends and these dividends will grow rapidly as you are propelled toward the successful achievement of your Vision.

If you invest some of your time to understand your Core Values, develop clarity by defining your life's Vision and create focus on the Long Term Goals necessary to reach them, you will be on your way to taking control of your TMP.

Time Management is not really about time at all. It's all about you and how you manage yourself and the activities in your life. Time Management is all about choices. Your entire life is made up of choices. Sometimes you will choose wisely and sometimes you will choose poorly. However, you will <u>always</u> have a choice. Right or wrong, always learn from the choices you make and you will do a better job of adding to your TMP.

If your goals are clearly defined and you are striving to achieve them you will be amazed at how many "lucky breaks" you will create for yourself. SMART Goals will help you to stay on the right path and enable you to take advantage of these opportunities that come along without getting sidetracked.

*"First, have a definite, **clear** practical ideal;
a goal, an objective. Second, have the
necessary means to achieve your ends;
wisdom, money, materials, and methods.
Third, adjust all your means to that end."*

Aristotle

FlightPath to Success™

So far we've discussed three key areas that will help you in your efforts to build up your TMP.

You have reviewed your personal Value system and you now have an enhanced understanding of why you make the choices you make and why you sometimes feel frustrated when you don't get as much accomplished as you planned.

You have taken a long look at where you would like to be in your ideal future and have a better understanding of what this Vision of your future looks like.

You should have spent a significant amount of time creating Long Term Goals that will keep you focused on key areas of this ideal future; and you now understand that there are very specific actions that you need to take in order to be successful. Together, these three steps are extremely important since they form the foundation of good Time Management.

Keep reminding yourself that doing what is most important *to you* is what allows you to accomplish more in less time.

We're now going to discuss how you can get better control of your daily activities. It is at this level that most people lose control of their time. Yet, it is at this level that we live and breathe. Everyone, every where lives in the present; not days, weeks, months and years into the future.

To assist you in understanding this principle, please refer to the diagram on the next page. After all, a picture is worth a 1,000 words. This illustration explains the correlation between what you believe in and what you want to get out of life; your Values & Vision, and how, your Goals, Objectives & Tasks will keep you headed in the right direction and provide you the structure needed to manage your time effectively. I call this *FlightPath to Success*™

"If one advances confidently in the direction of his dreams, and endeavors to live the life which he has imagined, he will meet with success unexpected in common hours."
Henry David Thoreau

For a larger, printable version of this
graphic, please visit our website:
www.performancegains.com

Here is a summary of the five different levels in the previous illustration. Some of this will serve as a review.

Core Values.

At the first level, the foundation of this process, identify your Core Values. These represent your deep rooted beliefs. They determine how and why you make the choices in your life. When decisions are made in harmony with your Core Values, life is good! You feel happy, satisfied, fulfilled and at peace with the world. However, when you make inappropriate or bad choices, or if outside events are in conflict with your Core Values, you feel threatened, unhappy, disappointed and out of control.

Generally you can identify 5 Core Values and your other Values will fall into one of these main categories. Now may be a great time to revisit your Core Values that were identified in chapter 2.

Your Vision.

At the second level is your Vision. Think of your Vision as a glimpse into the future - perfect in every way. It should encompass all your hopes, dreams and aspirations. In your perfect world you will achieve all you set out to accomplish by working hard and staying focused.

At the very least you will always strive for significant and meaningful goals that provide challenges.

Your Vision, when combined with your Values, will serve as your compass to keep you on course and always headed in the right direction. If you feel lost or uncertain where to go just revisit these areas and it will become perfectly clear.

Long Term Goals.

At the next level are your Long Term Goals. This is where your success strategy begins to take shape. I recommend that these Goals be 18-24 months into the future. Some people like a 3, 5 or 10 plan however, considering our rapidly changing world, this can be difficult for many people to comprehend. Regardless of how far out you plan, be certain that the Goals are achievable within your stated time frame and are directly connected to your Vision. In business, this level can become your "Mission Statement" because it clarifies your actions and expectations. I will leave it up to you to decide how far into the future you wish to plan.

Beating The Time Bandits

Short-Term Goals (Objectives).

This is level four. Here is where you take those big, seemingly impossible goals and begin to attack them. You do this by setting very specific short term (30-60-90 day) objectives that, when completed, will lead to accomplishing your Long Term Goal(s). While you may be working to achieve 4 or 5 Long Term Goals, you will have numerous Objectives that must be accomplished in order for you to ultimately achieve your Vision.

Daily Tasks.

At level five you have your Daily Tasks; often referred to as your To-Do List. Here is where you must fight the battle with the Time Bandits. You need to constantly ask yourself if you are engaged in activities (tasks) that lead directly toward the successful attainment of your goals. If you can answer "Yes," congratulations, you are making successful deposits into your TMP. If not than you are allowing the Time Bandits access to your account and losing valuable assets.

Notice how each of the five levels is connected to the level above and below? This is because for you to succeed in your battle with time and to make the maximum deposits

into your TMP all of these levels must be in harmony.
Whenever you find yourself wasting time or are feeling
overwhelmed, revisit the *FlightPath to Success*™ diagram
and see how your current activities fit in. You will discover
that you are engaging in activities that are not in your plan.
You are off your *FlightPath*. Bottom line - you are wasting
time!

*"The way to wealth, if you desire it, is as plain
as the way to market...waste neither time nor
money but make the best use of both"*

Ben Franklin

Many people and companies craft a Mission Statement to help define their direction. If you find this to be a useful tool by all means take the time to create one. I personally prefer a short and concise (10 words or less) Vision Statement and a Mission Statement to define the actions you will take to achieve it.

Below is what I believe to be an excellent example of a clear and concise Vision and Mission Statement.

The "Perfect" Vision and Mission Statement?

"Space, the Final Frontier –
These are the voyages of the
Starship Enterprise.
Its 5-year mission
to explore strange new worlds,
to seek out new life and civilizations,
to boldly go where no one has gone before."

Gene Roddenberry

As Dennis Miller would say: "Of course, this is just my opinion; I could be wrong"

To-Do Lists

I strongly urge everyone to use daily "To-Do" lists. It has been proven that this is one of the best ways to increase your productivity. The act of writing out what you want to do can decrease your implementation time by as much as 90%. So why wouldn't you do this? Over the years I have looked at and used numerous time management tools. This includes calendars, written planners, desktop planners, electronic planners, etc. Some worked and some didn't. In the end I believe it is best to find a system, any system that works for you and use it.

I believe to be effective any system must help you become a better time manager. What I really mean is that your system needs to help you prioritize what is most important to you at any point in time. Brian Tracy says that "…the biggest waste of time is doing well what need not be done at all." By knowing what is most important to you and your future, you will be able to answer the following question at any given point in time. The question to always be asking is: "If I could only do one thing right now that would have the greatest impact on my future, what would it be?" In other words, "How should I spend my time now?"

Beating The Time Bandits

Your TMP will grow in direct proportion to the actions you take in response to this question.

Here is a simple method I use to help determine my daily priorities.

1. At the end of each day, create a list of all the things you want to accomplish tomorrow.

2. Read the completed list for clarity and put it away. Allow your sub-conscious mind to "sleep on it."

3. When you begin your day in the morning, take out the list and prioritize it in the following manner.

Break down the list into three columns. The first column are "Must–Do" items; the items that will be completed by the end the day <u>without exception</u>. These items take you directly towards your objectives and goals; they represent the top 20% of your activities.

In the second column are your "Need To-Do" items. They represent high priority activities and also connect to your objectives and goals but are *not* urgent or critical. They represent about 50% of your activities.

Finally, in the last column list your "Nice To-Do" items." Just like the heading says, these items are nice to do. This column represents the remaining 30% of your activities, is the least productive (for you) and can get rather long.

Many people spend far too much time engaging in the

items from this section because they frequently represent the things you most enjoy doing. Fight this tendency and you will achieve much more success and eventually greater satisfaction. They offer little, if any, real return on your investment. Whenever possible, look to delegate or eliminate these completely from your daily routine. Don't worry; these items will move over to column 1 or 2 and get done if they become important enough.

Generally, the fewest number of items will appear in your "Must-Do" column since 80% of your results will come from 20% of your activities. This is the Pareto Principle, also known as the 80-20 Rule. It states that a small number of causes or activities (20%) are responsible for a large percentage (80%) of the effects or outcomes.

I'd like to make one final point about your "To-Do" list. We discussed at length the importance of living your Values and Vision and the impact this will have on increasing the value of your TMP. Here is a suggestion that can have a tremendous impact on your results.

Every day place at least one item in your "Must-Do" column that pertains to each of the major areas of your life. For example, if one of your major goals is to develop greater spiritual happiness, a "Must-Do" might be to read the bible for 10 minutes every day. If you want to build better relationships with your family, a "Must-Do" might be to tell every family member you love them and do it every day. Your "Must Do" items need not be huge to be effective but they must be relevant.

So far we have spent our time together discussing how you make your choices in life and by now you have a much clearer picture of where you are going in the days, weeks, months and years ahead. Hopefully you also comprehend that this thing called "time management" is not about how to squeeze more hours in your day that matters but it is about how you use the hours that you are given. Each and every moment is invaluable; if you think of time as money you will unquestionably invest it more wisely.

Here is what your list would look like.

Must Do	*Need To Do*	*Nice To Do*
These activities	Be certain	Only do these
return <u>80%</u>	these items are	activities if
of your results!	closely connected	everything else
	to your goals!	is completed

Remember, the time you spend on the Must Do items should account for 80% of your results! Try this for 30 days and track your progress. It will be substantial.

However, no matter how carefully you plan your activities, something or someone always seems to jump up and snatch some of it away. Just like a thief in the night can steal your wallet or purse; or a burglar can rob your house, the Time Bandits can steal your most valuable asset.

In the next chapter I will introduce you to the ten most notorious, sneaky and unscrupulous Time Bandits. But there is hope and you need not be defenseless; I promise to arm you with specific and proven defense tactics so you will no longer be at their mercy. I know how priceless time is so failure is not an option!

QUESTION:
How do you eat an elephant?

ANSWER:
One small bite at a time!

Beating The Time Bandits

Beating the Time Bandits

As discussed previously, you are the only person totally in charge of how you invest this valuable asset known as time. Everyone, every day has exactly the same amount of time and it is up to each of us to use it or lose it. Why is it that some people get so much accomplished while others seem to struggle just to make it through the day? Why is it that so many people end the day with more to do than when they started? So many people I work with feel tired, frustrated, and just plain worn out every day. No matter how hard they try they never seem to grow their TMP. They feel robbed.

This occurs because of the ongoing assault and attacks of the notorious Time Bandits. Just who are these sneaky, devious thieves that are responsible for draining countless numbers of Time Management Portfolios?

Allow me to introduce them to you and don't be surprised to discover that you are probably one of their many victims.

1. *Procrastination*
2. *Drop in visitors*
3. *Disorganization*
4. *Meetings*
5. *Perfectionism*
6. *Indecision*
7. *Poor Planning*
8. *Phone Distractions*
9. *E-Mail*
10. *Inability to Say "No"*

The Time Bandits

Do you recognize any of these Time Bandits? Most of them are probably familiar, yet we constantly allow them access to our TMP. We let them steal from our current assets and ultimately destroy our future.

Why do we permit this to continue? The reason we don't take control of our lives the way we should is because we become too accustomed to doing what other people want and forget about our own priorities. Or, we unknowingly believe it's easy or nobler to sacrifice what we want for what someone else wants. Once again, I am not implying that we should become selfish and unwilling to help others. What I am saying is we need to understand how and where other people's needs fit into our overall strategy. After all, our strategy is going to enable us to contribute the most to our TMP.

Let's take a closer look at the infamous Time Bandits and see if we can put some of them behind bars.

Beating The Time Bandits

Procrastination. Alias (AKA): Paulie the Procrastinator. We all know him. He appears whenever we don't want to do something. We have all kinds of reasons for avoiding the inevitable or disagreeable job facing us. *"It will take to long," "It's not something I enjoy doing," "I don't have everything I need to get started,"* etc. The truth is, most people procrastinate for one reason, fear. They are afraid to roll-up their sleeves and get started because they might fail. There is usually no basis for the fear but it is paralyzing and prevents them from taking action.

<u>Suggestions</u>:

1. Determine the worst possible outcome if you were to fail and commit to proceed courageously. Chances are failure will never be as bad as you imagine it to be.
2. Develop solutions to possible obstacles.
3. Identify and obtain all the available resources necessary to see the project through to completion.
4. Break down the project into small manageable pieces.

5. Prioritize the steps necessary for completion.

6. Determine specific dates for completion of each step.

7. Proceed one step at a time.

8. Reward yourself as you complete various stages of the project.

9. Start immediately.

"How wonderful it is that nobody need wait a single moment before starting to improve the world."

ANNE FRANK

Drop-in Visitors. Alias (AKA): Mary Popin. You know the scenario: You're in the midst of an important project or about to start a new one, and along comes Mary... *"Do you have a minute?"* she asks. And, you and I both know that with Mary, it's *never* just one minute! If you agree to the visit she snatches away a nice chunk of your TMP. What can you do?

<u>Suggestions</u>:

1. Stand up and greet her at the door before she comes in and makes herself at home. Don't give her an opportunity to get comfortable.
2. Politely explain this is *not* a good time and offer an alternative; this keeps you in control of the situation.
3. Keep your door closed when you don't want visitors and train your guests to honor this signal.
4. Don't become a Drop in Visitor yourself. Act the way you wish others to act.
5. If appropriate, face your desk away from the door to discourage people from grabbing your attention.

"The effectiveness of work increases according to geometric progression if there are no interruptions."
Andre Maurois

The Time Bandits

Disorganization. Alias (AKA): Debbie Disorganized. He wants to do well; but he just can't seem to find anything he needs. *"Where is that report?" "Has anyone seen my project file?"* He spends countless (and precious) hours preparing to do a 20-minute project; all because he doesn't have a system to get and stay organized.

Suggestions:

1. Set aside time today to get organized and this time do it (don't procrastinate!).
2. Use a personal organizer, paper or electronic, and keep it close at hand and use it.
3. Create a filing system that is simple but will work for you.
4. Buy lots of file folders and use them to organize and keep all relevant projects and similar information together.
5. Don't save everything you read just because you might use it someday.
6. When handling paper act on it, file it or discard it.
7. Avoid clutter in your work area (post it notes, scraps of paper with notes etc.)

8. When sorting mail and your inbox take action on small items immediately.

9. Keep your To Do list visible at all times and use it.

10. On a regular basis, schedule a small block of time to stay organized. This should be scheduled during "off hours" of your work week.

11. If you can't get yourself organized, find someone who can and hire them. It is cheaper than the alternative.

"The secret of all victory lies in the organization of the non-obvious."
Marcus Aurelius

The Time Bandits

Meetings. Alias (AKA): Mike the Meeting Man. Don't you just love hearing these words - *"We have a meeting in 20 minutes"?* Often this is one of the most notorious Time Bandits of all because he not only steals from you, but frequently he brings others along as well. Often this Bandit is a Kleptomaniac, someone who steals and doesn't know they are doing it. Do <u>you</u> schedule unproductive meetings? If you do; then you're the Bandit!

<u>Suggestions</u>:

1. Every meeting should have an agenda stating the purpose and time table.
2. Only relevant participants should be invited to attend.
3. Discussions should be limited to agenda items only; stay focused.
4. All participants should know their topics ahead of time and come prepared to participate.
5. Follow up minutes should be provided to all participants and others that have a stake in the outcome of meetings.
6. Start on time and end on time.

7. Schedule meetings before lunch or late on Friday; this will encourage people to get to the point quickly.

8. Avoid routine, regularly scheduled meetings unless they serve a real purpose.

9. There should always be one or more action plans created as a result of the meeting.

10. All participants need to be accountable for outcomes and commitments.

"I wasted time, and now doth time waste me."

William Shakespeare

Perfectionism. Alias (AKA): Paula Perfect. This particular Bandit is a master at reducing your TMP. He convinces you that *nothing* is ever good enough. It can always be just a little bit better. A brain surgeon must strive for perfection; on the other hand, many of your daily tasks can be done "well" and this will be more than sufficient. Do an excellent job when and if it is really necessary.

<u>Suggestions</u>:

1. Know what is needed to get the job done and do whatever is necessary; but don't overdo it.
2. If you're solving a problem, decide on the best workable solution and proceed.
3. Learn to know what results are necessary for a given task and apply the necessary effort instead of excessive effort.
4. Strive to do an excellent job, not a perfect job.

> *"Perfectionism is not a quest for the best. It is a pursuit of the worst in ourselves; the part that tells us that nothing we do will ever be good enough - that we should try again."*
> **Julia Cameron**

Indecision. Alias (AKA): Harry Hopeless. We've all met this guy. He thrives on uncertainty. Your best defense against Mr. Hopeless is a well thought out plan. A plan that is strategic and keeps you on track to your stated goals will hold him at bay. This bandit has a difficult time breaking in if you know what you want and how you're going to get it. He does his best work when you are "flying by the seat of your pants."

Suggestions:

1. Create a daily to do list and follow it.
2. Prioritize your list and do the important items first.
3. Make adjustments as long as they take you <u>closer</u> to your goals.
4. Use all your available resources.
5. Frequently ask yourself, "How should I spend my time <u>right now?</u>"

"Indecision may or may not be my problem."
                        Jimmy Buffett

Poor Planning. Alias (AKA): Charlie Chaos. Who needs a plan? Not this Bandit. He can do just about anything, on the fly, blindfolded. Right! Don't be fooled. Everyone can benefit from having a written plan. Research has proven that you can save as much as 90% of your implementation time just by creating a written plan.

Suggestions:

1. Your plan should reflect your Vision. It should be a key element in attaining your Long Term Goals.
2. Write out your plan.
3. Share it with those that will help you achieve your goals.
4. Hide it from anyone that will dissuade or discourage you.
5. Follow the plan.
6. Make adjustments as long as they take you <u>closer</u> to your goals.

"Let our advance worrying become advance thinking and planning."
        Winston Churchill

Beating The Time Bandits

Phone Distractions. Alias (AKA): Donna Diversion. You have a plan to get a lot accomplished today. You even manage to keep most of your Time Bandits at bay. You're actually making good progress and today is going to be a great success, but then ... _rrrringgg, rrringgg,_ the phone rings and you take the call. Alas, another Bandit escapes with your funds. You just have to answer every call that comes in, don't you? Or do you?

Suggestions:

1. Change your message and inform callers that you are in a meeting and will return at XX time. By the way, the "meeting" is with a very important client, YOU.
2. Tell callers you will return all calls between X and X PM - and do it.
3. Use call screening. After all, everyone else does why shouldn't you?
4. Consider the caller's real needs (their filters). If you must take a call, inform the caller that another time (you specify when) would be better and they will have your undivided attention.
5. Have someone take your calls for you.

6. When making important calls, plan ahead. Create an agenda and share it with the other person to accomplish more in less time.

7. Avoid needless socializing during work hours.

8. Teach callers how to use voicemail appropriately. Instruct them to tell you what they need and not just request a "call back." Frequently problems can be resolved without playing "phone tag"

"Telephone, n. An invention of the devil which abrogates some of the advantages of making a disagreeable person keep his distance."

Ambrose Bierce

E-Mail. Alias (AKA): Johnny Junk Mail. Johnny is a relatively new but one of the most cunning criminals of the 21st century. Electronic Mail! How did you <u>ever</u> survive without E-Mail? The answer is simple; you did fine. Remember our little FedEx story? If you are constantly checking your email every time the little voice says, "You've got mail;" whose lenses are you looking through? Generally speaking, 70-80% of your email will not be so urgent that you must respond instantly.

<u>Suggestions</u>:

1. Turn off the alert that informs you every time a new message arrives.
2. Train yourself to check your mail only 3-4 times daily. Try this schedule: when you first arrive at work, just after lunch and finally 60-90 minutes before ending your day. This will give you time to address anything that is really urgent.
3. Read the mail, follow up if appropriate; or delete it.
4. Learn to use your email client's (Outlook, ACT, Goldmine, Mozilla, etc.) built in tools for managing your mail.
5. Get a good Spam Filter.

The Time Bandits

Inability to say "NO" Alias (AKA): Dan the Door Mat. This is perhaps one of the coldest and most deceptive criminals of them all. This guy is always lying in the shadows ready to attack. He is so deadly because every time you can and don't say "*no*," all the other Bandits pile on and you lose. You need to know what is important to you, so you can comfortably and confidently say "NO" when you are asked to do things that are taking you away from your goals.

Suggestions:

1. Learn to say NO whenever you will be diverted from your plan.

2. Learn to say NO to yourself. There are times when you must decide what you are going to do and what you will not do. It is okay to say no to anything that is in conflict with your Core Values and stated Vision and Goals.

3. Offer alternatives when it is necessary to say no.

> *"Self-respect is the fruit of discipline; the sense of dignity grows with the ability to say **no** to oneself."*
> **Abraham J. Heschel**

Beating The Time Bandits

Obviously there is no single defense for fighting every Time Bandit; however, recognizing them is a good start.

Take time to review this chapter a second time. Commit to arresting one Time Bandit every day for the next 21 days. You will quickly see your TMP begin to grow. Once you have succeeded in eliminating a Bandit, go after another until you are at last in charge of your time.

Oh, by the way, if you didn't notice, frequently you may possess multiple personalities. YOU may assume any of the Time Bandit roles at a moments notice. In other words you are the Time Bandit!

When this occurs, it is up to you to take charge and stop the Time Bandit in his tracks.

"The average American worker has fifty interruptions a day, of which seventy percent have nothing to do with work."
W. Edwards Deming

Beating The Time Bandits

Bandit Proof Strategy

In the last chapter we discussed the top ten Time Bandits and offered suggestions for arresting them. You may have noticed that these bandits tend to hang out in the workplace however; upon closer examination you will see they really do attack us in our personal lives just as frequently. For instance, have you ever taken time to call a family member or close friend and after a few minutes of stimulating conversation you hear the infamous call waiting signal? What do you do? Chances are you at least click in to see who it is. If you do, a Time Bandit has struck again!

Take a closer look at the Time Bandits and see how many you can identify in your *personal* life and begin today to set up the appropriate defenses.

There is one additional Time Bandit defense I would like to share with you. In many ways I believe it to be your best overall defense. Here is the concept.

Most people, especially individuals that are working hard to provide for their future and the future of their families utilize some type of organizer or planner. It may be a day planner or calendar, electronic organizer in the form of Microsoft Outlook, ACT, a PDA or a combination of two or more of these. Regardless of the method, it has been my experience many people have become adept at planning their *business* activities. True, many of these people add personal items to their schedules but their work activities take priority. (I know several people that keep two planners, one for business and one for their personal life. I am not a proponent of this since my personal and professional lives have one thing in common; me, so one planner is just fine.) However, these same people often have another thing in common. They want desperately to have more time for themselves and their families. The problem: They don't have enough time. They would love to be able to take the kids to soccer or baseball practice; they wish there was enough time to go to the school play; and, they will, just as soon as they catch-up at the office, do all these things and much, much more! Sound familiar?

Let me offer a solution. I call the concept "*Backfilling your schedule.*" Here's how it works.

Take out a blank calendar for the coming 90 days. Sit down with your family and loved ones. Together, fill in all the upcoming activities and together make decisions on which ones you will attend; additionally, plan some new activities together. Also schedule some "me" time; time for you to recharge your batteries. Mark all these on your calendar, and transpose them to your planner as appointments. Once you have done this your planner is now ready to be "*Backfilled*" with your work related activities. Do not take these appointments lightly. Do not think you can just cancel or reschedule them because they're not real appointments. Not only are the important, they are probably your *most* important appointments. After all, they are with the key people in your life; yourself and your family!

If you follow this process and stick to your promises, you will see a dramatic decrease in the number of Time Bandit attacks on your TMP. Try it, it works!

"True success is the active pursuit of worthwhile goals"

Earl Nightingale

Summary

We are at the end of our journey so let's summarize what we discussed.

- Time really is your most valuable asset; it needs to be closely guarded and must never be taken for granted.
- Creating a *Time Management Portfolio* (TMP) will help you invest your time wisely and create immeasurable wealth and happiness.
- Managing your time means defining and understanding your *Core Values* and "seeing" the world through your eyes, not someone else's.
- Create a clear *Vision* of your future so you always know your final destination.
- Develop *Short* and *Long Term Goals* to keep you headed in the right direction.
- Set your goals using the *SMART* Goal Setting process to ensure success.
- You are surrounded by Time Bandits waiting to deplete your TMP unless you take steps to arrest them.

Beating The Time Bandits

- Setting priorities, your *Daily Tasks*, is a key weapon in your defense against the Time Bandits.
- You are one person; your personal and business life have one thing in common – _You_. Plan your business life to *complement* your personal life not *dominate* it.
- Time Management has little to do with time and *everything* to do with your choices.

Ultimately, whether you succeed or fail it is totally up to you and the choices you make. Choose wisely and you can beat your *Time Bandits*. I hope you found this book helpful and I wish you *Success, Wealth* and True *Happiness* in all of your life choices.

If you would like to learn more about Performance *GAINS* and how we can help you, visit or website: www.performancegains.com, or call us at 847.490.8402. We would be delighted to hear about your success!

PEACE
Bob Hartung

APPENDIX

I.   Time Bandits Arrest Warrants
II. Determine your Core Values
III. Create Your Vision Statement
IV. SMART Goal Setting Worksheets

Copies of these and additional tools are available free at our website: www.performancegains.com

Beating The Time Bandits

Time Bandits Arrest Warrant

On the following pages are forms to help you identify and arrest your Time Bandits.

Take time today to create plans to beat them and add to your Time Management Portfolio. Identify each of your personal Time Bandits and commit to a strategy to arrest them starting today. Begin with your biggest Bandit first as it will pay the biggest dividends into your account.

1. Name the Bandit or Bandits in each category.
2. Identify how much Time is being taken from you or what you are being prevented from accomplishing.
3. Indicate action steps to eliminate the Bandit.
4. Set a deadline to accomplish your goal.

NOTES

Time Bandits Arrest Warrant

Wanted
Paulie the Procrastinator

Description - Causes you to become frozen with fear preventing you from taking action on important goals and projects.

Name this Bandit in your life _____

_____

This Bandit is stopping me from _____

1. _____

2. _____

3. _____

4. _____

5. _____

I will stop this Bandit by taking the following Action Steps

1. _____

2. _____

3. _____

4. _____

5. _____

I will arrest this Bandit on or before _____

_____

<u>NOTES</u>

Time Bandits Arrest Warrant

Wanted
Mary Popin

<u>Description</u> - AKA - The uninvited guest. Always stops by for meaningless chatter or just to say hello and never leaves!

Who are these Bandits in your life

These Bandits are stopping me from
1.
2.
3.
4.
5.

I will stop these Bandits by taking the following Action Steps
1.
2.
3.
4.
5.

I will arrest this Bandit on or before

<u>NOTES</u>

Time Bandits Arrest Warrant

Wanted
Debbie Disorganized

<u>Description</u> – Never knows where anything is, spends most of her time looking for information *you* need to complete your job.

Who are these Bandits in your life
These Bandits are stopping me from
1.
2.
3.
4.
5.
I will stop these Bandits by taking the following Action Steps
1.
2.
3.
4.
5.
I will arrest these Bandits on or before

Beating The Time Bandits

NOTES

Time Bandits Arrest Warrant

Wanted
Mike the Meeting Man

<u>Description</u> – Schedules last minute meetings, meetings with no real purpose or agenda; invites everyone whether their needed or not.

Who are these Bandits in your life
_____

_____

These Bandits are stopping me from
_____

  1. _____

  2. _____

  3. _____

  4. _____

These bandits cost me approximately ___ hours each month
_____

I will stop these Bandits by taking the following Action Steps
_____

  1. _____

  2. _____

  3. _____

  4. _____

_____

I will arrest these Bandits on or before
_____

_____

<u>NOTES</u>

Time Bandits Arrest Warrant

Wanted
Paula Perfect

<u>Description</u> – Everything needs to be done perfectly; no exceptions and regardless of the cost in time and money, just do it until it's PERFECT!

Who are these Bandits in your life

These Bandits are stopping me from

   1.

   2.

   3.

   4.

   5.

I will stop these Bandits by taking the following Action Steps

   1.

   2.

   3.

   4.

   5.

I will arrest these Bandits on or before

<u>NOTES</u>

Time Bandits Arrest Warrant

Wanted
Harry Hopeless

<u>Description</u> – Never can make a choice; has the unique ability to delay every project while he gathers more and more information and still can't make a decision.

Who are these Bandits in your life

These Bandits are stopping me from

1.

2.

3.

4.

5.

I will stop these Bandits by taking the following Action Steps

1.

2.

3.

4.

5.

I will arrest these Bandits on or before

NOTES

Time Bandits Arrest Warrant

Wanted
Charlie Chaos

<u>Description</u> – AKA: Mr. Fly by the seat of his pants. Always reacts, never thinks or plans ahead

Who are these Bandits in your life
_____

_____

These Bandits are stopping me from
_____

  1. _____

  2. _____

  3. _____

  4. _____

  5. _____

I will stop these Bandits by taking the following Action Steps
_____

  1. _____

  2. _____

  3. _____

  4. _____

  5. _____

I will arrest these Bandits on or before
_____

_____

<u>NOTES</u>

Time Bandits Arrest Warrant

Wanted
Donna Diversion

Description – Endlessly disrupts the work flow with "urgent" calls. Poor voice mail skills.

Who are these Bandits in your life _____

_____

These Bandits are stopping me from _____

1. _____
2. _____
3. _____
4. _____
5. _____

I will stop these Bandits by taking the following Action Steps _____

1. _____
2. _____
3. _____
4. _____
5. _____

_____

I will arrest these Bandits on or before _____

_____

<u>NOTES</u>

Time Bandits Arrest Warrant

Wanted
Johnny Junk Mail

<u>Description</u> – AKA – "You've got mail." Sends countless urgent communications 24/7. Often the subject line says: "You've just got to see this!" or "FW: FW: FW: FW: Re: ... "

Who are these Bandits in your life

_____

These Bandits are stopping me from

1. _____
2. _____
3. _____
4. _____
5. _____

I will stop these Bandits by taking the following Action Steps

1. _____
2. _____
3. _____
4. _____
5. _____

I will arrest this Bandit on or before

_____

<u>NOTES</u>

Time Bandits Arrest Warrant

Wanted
Dan the Door Mat

Description – They allow others to make their choices and do little at all to manage their own priorities; never have time for themselves.

Who are these Bandits in your life   (Hint: Kleptomaniac)
_____

These Bandits are stopping me from
_____
   1. _____
   2. _____
   3. _____
   4. _____
   5. _____

I will stop these Bandits by taking the following Action Steps
   1. _____
   2. _____
   3. _____
   4. _____
   5. _____

I will arrest these Bandits on or before
_____

NOTES

Determine Your Core Values

Name your Role Models; What do you Admire about them?

List your Top Core Values

Identify your Top Five Core Values

1.
2.
3.
4.
5.

Beating The Time Bandits

Vision Statement

First Draft of your Vision Statement

_____

_____

_____

_____

_____

_____

_____

_____

_____

_____

_____

_____

_____

_____

_____

_____

Beating The Time Bandits

Second Draft of your Vision Statement

_____

_____

_____

_____

_____

_____

_____

_____

_____

_____

_____

_____

_____

_____

_____

_____

_____

_____

_____

_____

Beating The Time Bandits

Final Version of Your Vision Statement

_____

_____

_____

_____

_____

_____

_____

_____

_____

_____

_____

_____

_____

_____

My Vision in 10 words or less

_____

_____

_____

Beating The Time Bandits

SMART Goal Setting

SMART Goals

S.M.A.R.T. Goals will help you achieve more in less time. They will keep you on track, focused and help you create significant and meaningful results.

Follow this simple 5-step process.

Goals need to be <u>Specific</u> – To have the greatest impact; all Goals must be stated in very specific terms.

Part of this specificity includes some form of measurement. Stating your Goal using measurable terms will help you track your progress good or bad, and will act as a compass to keep you headed in the right direction.

Avoid vague and ambiguous words like "better" or "improve." Instead state what "better" is (increase my income $5000 more than last year) or (maintain a 50% improvement over the last quarter.)

Research shows that when activities are measured, results increase.

On the next page, create your Goal using the above format.

Beating The Time Bandits

SMART Goal Setting

My GOAL

_____

_____

_____

_____

_____

_____

_____

_____

_____

_____

_____

_____

_____

_____

_____

_____

_____

_____

Beating The Time Bandits

Goals need to be <u>Meaningful</u> - If you are going to achieve your goal and become successful you are going to work hard and make sacrifices. Therefore, there must be something in it for you!

What will be your reward for accomplishing this goal?

How will you be changed?

What are the ramifications of not completing this goal?

You need to fully understand and desire the *benefits* of achieving your goal.

On the following page, make a list of the positive outcome(s) of reaching your goal and the consequences of inaction or failure.

Using this information, create an accurate visualization of the successful completion of your goal.

SMART Goal Setting

Benefits	Consequences

Visualization Statement of my Goal

On a daily basis, refer to this visualization to stay focused on your Goal and to maintain your motivation.

Goals need to be <u>Achievable</u> – Meaningful Goals require sacrifice; they require you to go outside of your comfort zone and cause you to "stretch." If you will achieve something by just "showing up" it is not really a goal. However, you should avoid the tendency to reach to high, to fast thereby creating failure and disappointment. This is de-motivating and, constant failure will cause you to lose your desire to win.

On the following page, take time to consider all the possible obstacles to achieving your Goal and then develop solutions for them.

On your journey of Goal achievement, you will of course encounter problems; however, this exercise will help you maintain focus and be prepared with solutions.

SMART Goal Setting

Obstacles	Solutions

Beating The Time Bandits

You need to commit <u>Resources</u> to achieve you Goals– What knowledge and skills will you need to acquire and what people can you engage in order to help you achieve your goal? What financial commitments and personal sacrifices must you make to successfully complete your goal?

Take time to think this through and create a plan to use *everything* and *everyone* at your disposal. If appropriate, create two realistic budgets.

One based upon the total amount of time that will be required to reach your goal. Is it hours? Days? Weeks?

Second, create a financial budget based on commitments that may be required.

SMART Goal Setting

Knowledge I need to acquire

_____

_____

_____

Skills I need to learn

_____

_____

_____

_____

People I need to know

_____

_____

_____

Time Budget

_____

_____

Financial Budget

_____

_____

_____

Goals need to be <u>Time Definite</u> – Goals have a beginning and an end; they are ACTION Orientated. List every step needed from now until completion. Include dates, times, places, tasks, etc. for each item and then prioritize this list. This becomes your Action Plan.

Follow it until the completion of your goal.

Keep in mind that the resources allocated to achieve the goal can significantly impact your time-lines.

On the following page, create your Action Plan

SMART Goal Setting

Action Plan

What	Who	When
List the specific tasks to be completed	People Involved	Specific Deadline

Beating The Time Bandits

Acknowledgements

Throughout my career I have been blessed with great business associates and mentors. While with Sears, Larry Davis, Dave Steiger, Ed LaBelle, Elda Friedman, George Wisk and in particular my close friend of 28 years, Jesse Lee, all helped to get me started on the right foot and I am forever in their debt.

In my "second career," my days in the transportation industry, I learned many valuable lessons from Bart Theile and Al Redszus.

From my early days in consulting, Joe Kistner, Dr. Michael Koch, Jeff Percival, Dave Bruno, Jim Velos and Doug Blanchard were great resources and provided valuable insights and encouragement; I thank you all.

I have also learned countless lessons from my affiliations with HRD Press Training House, M1, Maximum Potential, William Mills & Associates, and of course, Nightingale Conant.

Lastly, several people have greatly influenced me on a personal level. They include my parents, grand parents (I miss you all), and my good friend Bill Schenck.

To everyone else that has influenced me you have my heartfelt thanks and never-ending gratitude. Together you have made me what I am today.

Beating The Time Bandits

Beating The Time Bandits